Constellations

IAN PINDAR was born in London in 1970. He published ... first work, a life of James Joyce, in 2004. *Emporium*, his debut poetry collection, appeared in 2011. *Constellations* is his second collection. His poems have appeared in *The English Review*, *The Forward Book of Poetry 2011* and *2012*, *London Magazine*, *Magma*, *New Poetries III*, *Oxford Poetry*, *PN Review*, *Poetry Review*, *Stand*, the *Times Literary Supplement* and *Wave Composition*. Pindar won second prize in the National Poetry Competition 2009, a supplementary prize in the Bridport Prize 2010 and was shortlisted for the 2010 Forward Prize (Best Single Poem). He lives in Oxfordshire.

Also by Ian Pindar from Carcanet Press

Emporium

IAN PINDAR

Constellations

First published in Great Britain in 2012 by

Carcanet Press Limited
Alliance House
Cross Street
Manchester M2 7AQ

www.carcanet.co.uk

Copyright © Ian Pindar 2012

A CIP catalogue record for this book is available from the British Library

ISBN 978 1 84777 096 7

The publisher acknowledges financial assistance from Arts Council England

Typeset by XL Publishing Services, Tiverton
Printed and bound in England by SRP Ltd, Exeter

to the Carpenter

Acknowledgements

My thanks to Michael Schmidt and Chris Hamilton-Emery, Judith Willson and everyone at Carcanet. Thanks are also due to the editors of *The English Review*, *Poetry Review* and *Wave Composition*, where some of the poems in *Constellations* first appeared in slightly different forms. I am grateful to A.P. Watt Ltd on behalf of The Literary Executors of the Estate of H.G. Wells for permission to quote from *The Time Machine* on p. 104. As always, Ali, Izzy and Tom graced me with their days.

Constellations

I

1

Sweetness, some cloudlessness, some shapes,
a random horse, the rolling arrangement
of the mind, with open eyes.

Fluttering gold limbs of brown leaves
sunned by straight cloudless blue in October,
bits and pieces of the sometimes Sunday.

A real skyline for its own sake.
Not regret in the sky but late light,
little certainty in the dusk.

Old cars and roses. The yard prepares for evening.
It knows the colour of yesterday,
as the shapes in the yard are angles of themselves.

This night of royal blue can taste the sea,
reflected in a field of smoothness,
gulls tumbling over the tide.

The tide goes out, the tide comes in.
Everything seems to want to be
electric. Everything comes alive.

2

The multiple appearances of the world,
the shapes it makes, a succession of organic forms,

of breaths of irreducible beings, the breath
that hesitates between the haunted and the painted.

Flower, landscape, portrait, self-portrait.
Humans, plants, animals, manifestations

of the question, finite nuances of nature,
numerous ripples and representations of forms,

muscle, flesh, bone, breath, the expressionless
coolness of the day, capturing colour

and light, the life of rain, the secret surging
of the sea. The sea lay soft on the rocks,

covering its modesty with north-east spray,
the rocks at the end of the world, the ships on the water,

the vessels of the years passing, the morning on its wings
of geography, pink and grey, incoming tide

of events, the boats still waiting to be free,
the harbour of local genealogies,

of local lives and loves, the finite progress
of great and small, the personal impersonal.

3

The place lies open to the elements,
the elements of creation. The focus
of the wind changes everything,
the weather a white flash. The mountains witness

this whiteness and present themselves as hybrids,
half-stone, half-water, while back and forth
go the clouds, their soft gymnastics.
Simple those summer days. In the sun,

under the sun, the whole body trembling,
the whole field of the body dreaming
in ferocious heat, certain moments sleepy
in outline but bright and smooth in gliding streams

of light beyond the realm of the figure. The force
that breaks through is brilliant, mixed and created fire,
so after slush and cold, chilly dark and deep,
come wavering threads of blossom and bloom.

The concupiscence of spring, the shimmering of summer,
the fullness of autumn, the ceremony of winter,
each landscape looks at them differently,
each landscape a playground for the years.

4

The horizontal heat of summer. The sun
on the balcony, twitching its pattern,
patterning the circle of contemplation.

To turn into what we watch, or below the flowers
to stretch and look again and appreciate
the approach of morning, the awakening shell,

the opaque belly of the sleeping body, the discovery
of the small of the back, the burnished glory
of the old treasury, the treasure trove,

thoughts on love and joy and momentaneity.
The movement follows you as the daytime sleeps,
the rooftop light and confusion, the abandoned folds

of the view, the senses half-engaged
in a half-fallen reality, the light
crumbling around it. Today is today.

5

Summer is already understood,
is already literature. A sweet coolness
creates a concert of concrete senses,

scent and light, flight and felicity,
a new language. Lost in the faraway,
the loved landscape cannot love. The love

of life that is a mode of poetry
gives back to humanity in chains.
Prisoners of memory remember too much.

Immense world of immense significance to us,
of which the immense cosmos is scarcely aware,
the Earth is almost immortal, almost timeless;

one could almost forget the same star that warms it now
and brings it life, expends upon it the most expansive,
auspicious, unerring, encircling light, will one day

boil away the oceans. The shifting skies are not
immortal, the living are not, nor the lakes
and hours and bars and restaurants and daylight and laughter.

6

A summer's day of images, a field of fire,
the blue beautiful, the morning so clear,

so innocent, sitting in a rocking chair
reading Baudelaire, the path of the day

so exposed, a revelation. The afternoon light
still clinging, leading us across the sky

towards evening, towards a moment when
the others are disburdened, talking in the garden

in habitable forms of kindness, agreeable natures,
no calculation or discouragement, no hate

but serene, friendly, almost fantastic, filling
the reality with feeling, with integrity,

complete in each other, full of sexualised ideas
picked up at random and grown in small flats and cafés.

7

We are completely physical, as thoughts are physical
and we are always thinking, champions of ourselves

in our field, a cry to the contrary of our beginning.
To achieve ourselves. To become an answer to ourselves

as question. To move freely and answer the soft
folds of flesh, the light itself, as the light

questions the interval, the unenlightened. To bend
reality and break with tradition, a community

of experiment, something like the beginning
of an allegiance. To recover the wonder. To follow

the world in its glassy shimmer, the safe haven
of every day, the benefaction of the morning,

the almost tender dawn, the sharp salt breezes,
the burning sun, the clamour of all this light.

The frame slips in search of a feature, the whole
of that slumbrous, sunny fragment of frame.

8

It is a light that causes abstractions,
itself an abstraction, orange-gold,
supporting nothing, nothing orange or gold,

or greenish-blue. It is an independent
vision of a period, a portrait
of the artist as an atmosphere.

The following winter, more crisply delineated,
the surfaces of light resemble
a profusely patterned fabric of branching veins.

A change of viewpoint. These movements correspond
to different movements of the eye
and effects of fragmentation.

The light here is filled with transitions
and wild distortions, the broken rays
of the sun shouting between the trees,

beneficent star of accidental bounty.
The effect is very free
and very freeing and incomplete.

II

10

When bicycles come down the lane,
trailing bright sunny faces,
you should wave at the women in blue dresses

who have not travelled far beyond their region,
but know how to love in cotton cardigan caresses,
sleeves of blue cardigans rolled to the elbow,

sensible hair and strong features,
strong arms and strong legs and thighs,
they rise to pass you and fix you with sensible eyes.

The countryside is on their side.
The lane is reliable in good weather
and leads them wherever they would go.

11

When the surrounding light changes, it obtains
a certain balance, leaving impressions of colour,
the colour of comparison. Then a moment comes
when all is incomparable: pure difference.

We want to recognise the new when it arrives,
beginning and beginning again,
but the new is always unrecognised
and cannot become established as 'the new'.

The wooded hills never stopped being new.
The river is very wide and seems
to lend itself to the new, becoming a place
where newness returns and passes through.

12

There is so much to resist, but this says 'Come.'
The river a flow, a process, to be happy
here is not denied us. The surprise

of laughter, the apple's firmness,
the skies launched in flowers of unconstrained doves,
good fortune of good graces on the run.

The guest at rest in the passageway, the mind
at work in the house, the deep, rhythmic sleep
of the darling, the colour of admiring her,

the same bright openness of this beauty.
A portrait or snapshot reality. At the window,
accurate stems of accurate flowers.

13

In love with love, amorous intellects,
flirtatious, bright and laughing, pace

the riverside apartment where luxurious
flowers full of warmth and energy,

glittering, so voluptuous, ebullient,
living in a land of water, a land

of pale green, their ruby-red resonance
ripened by reconciliation,

a flower-stem fortress of innocent fortitude
and inner glory. Golden sunlight suggests

a dream, the coloured backdrop animated by
their new feelings, and it is beautiful.

14

Being in love, being for the other, wrapping
the other in a brief life, a brief heat

of moment, a preposterous moment: the present,
an undimmed, undaunted meanwhile.

The self realised in time, bound to the present,
bound to a character, bound to be abandoned.

The same night in all of us, an end
and a beginning, each new life refining the real.

15

They see each other better with eyes closed, dreaming
of tenderness, the brief erotic life of her hand on his,

the murmur of substance, a body bestowed, an index
of contraction and expansion, a possibility with memories,

motives, desires, a direction, ourselves alone,
our own things, our reputations, our dangers, our associations,

our visions, our health, our explorations, our instinct;
amorous government officials, priests, amorous streets

and episodes, crowds and dancing, beautiful events,
the most beautiful, sex, love, the phases of the moon,

the arms of lovers, immovable armies of friends,
sympathy among the crowd, sympathy in the sky.

16

Long sunsets sometimes, smoke sometimes, air.
The river sings downstream, upstream,

beside the house of good manners,
where cheerful human figures, withdrawn

from the wind, drift and dream, voices,
many voices speaking with one voice.

What happens arranges a thought in a becoming.
It is an age. A subject for sky.

17

The sky gathers innocence
in praise of acres and bright houses,
where bright parrots squawk at quivering windows
and violas play in upstairs rooms.

We cannot own the day but we can play in it,
a willingness to travel, to transform
what wonders in occasional affairs
of scattered clothes, worth so much more than nothing,

to wear the moon or keep its shape about you,
to wear it as your own and name it,
to love your sleek appraisal of your own sleekness,
light-hearted, seeing the joke in your body's beauty.

18

There she is, in painted life,
the woman who took her clothes off for the painter.

He felt her vitality,
even when the woman dozed in the studio.

She brought him certainty, not in himself
but as a quantity of space and colour,

how she composed herself on the mini-proscenium,
shifted the robes he gave her, the ruffled robes,

how she would gather the tension in the room
in carefully staged abandon,

the certain form on which his uncertainties
foundered. She lived in the illusion of indolence,

where she would lie among patterned fabrics
and the contagious repetition of colour.

19

New vistas and visas, new rooms with new aromas.
This room smelling of green pine forest has never

seen a green pine forest but looks out over
the sea all mixed up outside. The seafront houses

also make no sense, blue and yellow,
green and red, assault the axiom of the eye,

a spectrum too abstruse. Harmony
preserves the sea and sky, the altered colour

of a final region, a conjoint realisation
of the truth, in which the unintelligible

and passing details are deceived in their passing.
Life is a holiday. From love and sudden joy,

the individual life of women and men,
the individual music, the good of the night.

20

They stayed a while. They read poetry.
They looked out of opposite windows. They bathed together.
They scrubbed themselves. They dressed for dinner.

They ordered fish. They ate fish. They noticed
when the overhead light flickered. They balanced on the wall
of the evening. They said 'I know,' 'I don't know.'

They folded their clothes. They threw down their clothes.
They lay together. They brushed their teeth. They banged
their knees on the night table. They went back to sleep.

They sat in deckchairs. They wrote postcards.
They applied suntan lotion. They both forgot
to pack a camera. They simply stared at the sea.

They paid for coffee and ice cream. They watched
the light turn over the sky in the square. They got lost.
They asked for directions. They limped back late, laughing.

21

These complications are the journey itself.
The complicated folds around the lovers
are their own limbs folded, streaked

with violent tones of blue, yellow and red,
the sheets implicated, being the universe,
being a moving scene, shaking a structure,

moving as never before, seen to be
still keeping, still changing position.
They take from one another a face

within reach, a double image,
reflecting upon its connecting spine,
its vertical vein, the opening of the centre,

the seductive endurance of the particular,
whatever occupies space and can be touched,
stroked, kissed, loved and held closer.

22

It is an act of love to affirm, to create
and connect, the sun warm on the window;

loving the sun, loving the arrival of the other,
their punctual particulars, points

and curves, their mathematical reality,
a different order of coordination,

a zone of exploration, the world
becoming smaller and more exclusive,

to disappear once again, to arrive,
as the moment jumps over the lifetime.

23

The love between two people is rare.
Mere juxtaposition is not enough.

Every relationship is fleeting
and requires sympathy.

To live with a beautiful oval face,
sometimes solemn and thoughtful or else

vague and inexpressive, to live
with grace and elegance in days

without grace or elegance is to be
beguiled by a form, filled with affection

and sensual delight, creating the illusion
of an everlasting vision and amour.

24

Or alone on the beach, in the heat, arms crossed, triumphant,
observing the visible shapes of visible things,
tangible, material:

the pink promenade and striped awnings,
shady, shared spaces filled with laughter.
They catch a mood, an intelligence, a problem

solved that kept us sad, that gave us such trouble.
There is a perfect far and wide, including
friendship, including love, including strangers,

including day and night. The sun puzzles
over stones, a crab, water, a wall.
It twinkles under sand. The sky is soft

and blank. The range of colours is extensive
and changes often, sometimes dissolving into
different shades or breaking into brightness.

25

The mellow beauty of smoke rising, the grace
of cobblestones and steep streets, the gulls
crossing the sun like a shutter, the local stone,

the arch of the bridge trembling between fullness
and emptiness, innocent and overflowing
waters of life. And high up from the sea, .

placid nature, the waves vague and absorbing,
enveloped in broad daylight, the various parts
speaking with one voice. The shining Earth,

the white annihilation of the sun,
its mysteries of heaven, the elusive sky,
celestial field of light, of lucency.

26

She makes watercolours of the *plage*
below the hotel terrace, where the water
brings colour, perspective, a coastline,

the ordinary details of wavering waves,
scarlet sails and the vivid sympathies
of rough-bordered huts and seaside façades.

It is an open energy, the eye
and hand exchanging their energy,
the passing of the day, the twitching brush

reconstructing a backdrop, building shapes,
the intermittent failures and forgivenesses,
incompetence a part of the design;

the declaration of an image, its figurative aspect,
not the scene itself but a record of its absence,
the maddening absence of reality;

the sand flat covered by standing water
at low tide, the sloping shadows where the eye
must choose between various types of sand,

as cumaceans and amphipods must understand
the different substrata or perish.
The back and forth of the brush, a difficult

furthering; intense, informal immediacy
the light seeping over the page,
the blue sky its legacy, the whole sky blue.

27

Luminous in love, a brief instant
on Earth, the young oak summoned by love,

enfolded in quivering flesh, enjoyed the intimate
illusion of flesh, the lingering insubstantiality

of the day. The daylight fades
in the swelling tide. The rhythm of the time

is the same, the shadows are the same,
they are moving, they are growing, they move up

the stairs, they are lost in the woods, prowl
the narrow streets, are stiff and knock together

in the shroud, the bed of death. The awakening sand,
blue under the moon, outliving day.

28

The Earth, the base of heaven without heaven,
is awake again, the world of flux a world of forms.

Hoteliers turn off their neon signs: THE ROYAL,
THE IMPERIAL, BELLEVUE, each private room a nest,

a darling mess in our off-centre world.
The body in its discipline of limbs

arranged in lazy patterns on the bed
is a throw of the dice, its own belle view

and miracle. Reflecting from the pillow
on white pillows crossing the pole

it seems obvious we are in space,
isolate and unspecified.

29

High, wavering light can hypnotise
the cool evening. Everything
it understands is abstract.

The green prematurely brown,
the brown prematurely grey
or white, a life of entire days.

Next year the dwindling light
will wobble and throw us over for
new guests, new newspapers

at breakfast and new faces, new hands
and feet on the staircases, fresh beds,
fresh sheets and new-fallen fruit.

III

30

When the bottom fell out of the market, the oranges
rolled down the hill, down the white lane.
Each orange existed in its own light,
complete in its geometry.

Old smiling men no longer smiled; their wives
wore black in the marketplace, the marketplace
an ancient splendour remembered through nights of cold.
After the passion of the oranges, it is as if

nothing indicates a world to come. They want
to return to lacemaking, chestnut-harvesting,
donkey-breeding, millinery. They want
the market to express its choice and turn

again with the seasons, turning a profit.
They have known the market and loved the market
or learned to love it and see it and follow it,
its movements, its misery, its mystery.

31

The fish in the market are strange.
They bear sad tidings and lie

on ice, mouthing their despair.
Eyes wide open, they look

surprised to be so glazed
and stunned, so horizontal.

The sea still moves inside them,
the mischievous, unconcerned ocean.

32

The land is black, grey on the hills, almost white.
The land will show you nothing, answer no question.

It resents nothing, needs no one.
No answer would suffice. No answer would undo

its white and black. No answer would bring colour
to the land. You have been in this land too long,

on the edge of this land, looking over it, into it.
You have prayed for everything that lives in it,

prayed for a strong current to wash it away,
to drown everything and told yourself it would be

a blessing, a blessing to force a change on the land,
this land so impassable, impossible.

33

The roads are lost and the old signs, and together
they named until now the image of a century.

The limit has fallen on all that befalls us.
The way that here and everywhere else

is everywhere else, an older order
could hardly understand. Everywhere

is nowhere and nowhere is everywhere.
We speak many languages,

a variety of yeses and nos,
a talking about, a talking around

definition, understanding clearly
the line must be clear, against intransigence,

the test of a language is a refusal to speak.
Peace and democracy travel together

and everything else is a distraction from
peace and democracy.

34

Meanings are disputed, nourished by conflict,
a world of fanatical meanings, the furthest from us,

statements in the news of West, of East,
claim and counter-claim of oil and gold,

business, daily business. How disciplines of meaning
discipline others, a military meaning

of barking dogs, stupefied, ugly,
full of repetitions and echoes. The victory of the echo.

35

Shooting began at dawn over the unburied,
in ripped fields of military renown.

We began dying, lost numbers, lost sight of it,
joining the crowded page of the dead. We may never

again see the sun rise over the unrivalled river,
our talkative town, the beehive residency

and last night we lost the support of reality.
Perfecting people is a bloody business.

36

A moon comes ashore and stays its quivering hand,
too light to be immense, too worldly to be
a theology, a feeling of the night,

of the leavings of understanding, a subtle glow.
The beggar and the white rock, the uniforms
and wrecked houses, the positions of the dead,

the dead positions, the shaking of the ground,
the beggar holding his lips tight together
and looking away. To turn and stretch, blaspheme,

look at the moon and far mountains,
holding the horse by the bridle. The mist like conversation,
a cold conversation on a mountainside.

37

Here are the things you miss: her green eyes,
her kisses, the house itself with its decorated glass,

the shops that seemed trivial before, that brown velveteen
coat you never wore, the British Museum pigeons,

newspapers, that white bowl in the middle
of the table, eggs, walking past churches, friends

and their children, intellectual passion, the cinema,
clowns, the Greek myths, books of poetry.

38

How methodical the nurses, how unhurried,
in grey and white, their humane purpose blooms
and persists in an age of so-called progress.

Women in their supreme generosity
come back into his life, sit by his bed
in silent contemplation, and later sit

on the train that carries him home after the slaughter,
over the tracks through meadows of riversweet water,
each eye of pasture connecting disaster to disaster.

39

Always the impulse to strive for feeling, for a new
cheerfulness, a kind of commonplace in days of creation,
so natural, growing ripe for happiness

in unaccustomed streets, something so obviously
something. Some creatures are human, similarities
of compounds, multitudinous brains and bubbles,

earthly individuals in stylistic and thematic
self-consciousness. A companion sometimes, shattered
impressions of indefinitely walking in time, talking

to another, under the influence, the apprehension, the difficulty
of meeting the mind of another, the grain of company.
A magnificent awareness of mind, of totality,

of existence acquired through repetition, but to discover
the laws of yourself, your own art, eyes of combination
and feeling, face to face movements of different-

coloured constitutions, the bright display,
the writing through colour, through irregularity,
the beauty of different parts, different arts.

40

The streets have a carnival atmosphere to shake
the Earth, a portrayal of exhilaration, sold out,

re-imagined and magnified illustrated ecstasies,
the last great auction of the old world, celebrated

by State poetry in language that is never
strangered, a world that belongs to maps and parchments,

the weapon of the book, the book of the conquest
to gratify the careful conquerors of the age,

the history of civilisation is a frame
of mind in architecture of proud bearing,

engraved names, chronicles, a sketch
of character in provincial brick and stone.

41

The streets are occupied by preoccupied creatures
full of monologues, colleagues of what's happening,

accurate geographers of mental maps, protagonists
of a living reality mistaken for an ordinary day.

Cafés and bars, the fear and magic of an age,
a portrait of the century in silver-grey; the dreams

of dead friends and people in public places,
moving at a relaxed pace, eyes and brains

and bodies in play, flowing in the mainstream,
on their faces mortal answers to mortal questions.

42

Creation is the challenge. To resist
the current order and find delight in living.

The fathers, the old forbidding fathers,
dead fathers of discipline and deference,

sterilise and paralyse, impose
a style and call it the law, a code to be

repeated in a culture that repeats.
Always an order—fixed, fatal reflux

of repetition—to police the swarming
chaos of the mind's mutation.

43

The differences undo us, affirming life
in its complexity, without finding

sameness in the other, in otherness,
without calling everything that changes 'evil'

and the nothing at all that stays the same 'good'.
Some struggle to stay the same. We struggle to change.

44

Continuity is its own outcome,
overcoming the gaps in time of human

experience. It makes a composition,
a philosophy out of the single-minded

version we observe; mistaking the uncertain
successions of things for certainty.

The history of novelty is a long one,
despite expectations of sameness occurring.

45

The past will not keep you
and you do not exist in the future.

You charm the present moment.
What saves you is the now.

The finite certainty: no time
and more than enough

to move and dream enough
to force a strange enchantment.

46

The sun on a bowl on a table in a house
populated by the sun, a glint
of white, a flash of forgotten origin.

The outside chewing up the day,
blue sea and clouds, and the smell of year
after year. All the materials of a self.

All the materials of a self
in temporary alignment,
an alliance of old and new,

a self in transition, working
to invent itself, a passage
from nothing to something and back.

47

All the inherited fields and grounds
of formulation, formulating words

of being, are provisional.
The play of production displaces

the chain of being, and depth and noise
give way to silence and surface.

48

There is a destination for those who recover
meaning, for those who want to know the sequel

to everything, the prequel to everything, but for those for whom
the origin is a sort of nonsense we borrow the surface,

the sensibility of the object, the unthinkable
freedom of the surface of things; we refuse to separate

the remains of everything from the context of its own light,
its narrow language, the drama of the dream.

49

A vision of falling or sleeping through time. No roots
to bear his dear life and no inheritance.

No command or voice of reason. Each came sleeping
to fall or fail at the feet of rooted reason.

Time you were good to us once, but once only.
We cannot go back for seconds. Time will not end

when our time ends. More sleepers will come
with more reasons to be sleepers among sleepers.

50

The dreams of separate dreamers come to rely
on reality, a shared reality,

a waking dream of the real made unreal by sleep;
a reality to which we might belong,

day and night, if we could but take upon
ourselves the burdensome reality

of making reality less burdensome,
a little lighter, please.

They supervise the sunlight in our day
but night belongs to dream,

the offhand abandon of impermanence,
the *son et lumière* of the dreamer.

51

He has a mind of blood and a hole to speak with,
a weight of organs around his heart, a head

in which to hatch and die. He has a mind
made up of other minds and knows the Earth

will swallow up all differences in disdainful
night. He likes his life. The fugue of plant

on dump is his destiny, but let him sing,
let him eat dates under a tree and remember.

52

The long apart forget themselves
in backward glances, in afternoons

of silent intimacy; at noon
a quiet inward space of a room

lost in time, the air binding
the atoms of dust, lust. It is about

nakedness, about nothing hidden.
The skin is itself, the room is itself,

the sea is itself, the sun on the sea
is itself, the vibrant light, the lustre.

53

The eye returns to see the sunshine, the golden year,
remembers the pleasing love of life,
marvellous voice of the nearest, the full feeling
of understanding, the fire of another,

an answer for all the rest. Things remain,
a stretched-out remembrance of cloth and colour,
the lasting flowers of memory, the most loved
looking back, the most moving. Provocation

of memory, proof of the moment, the white world
of a moment, the sun caught in the companion,
the whisper of the wind, the high rocks,
the wholesome foaming sea, the lives so young,

so deep the water, treading down into darkness,
the separating water, the elapsed time
of talking and changing. A long while past the ground
has no history, the world continues, the forgotten love

of breath of vision of joy, the remembrance of rich
articulate times of self-possibility,
an inference of endurance. The point of contact,
lovers of all times, patterns of loving,

forces of species, stimulating the situation of themselves
in mornings of impatient undisciplined desire,
a new synthesis. The round clarity of the moon,
the midnight tribute to heaven. The night-blue bodies

of outward inwardness, delightful, power
the pleasured interest, the thankful trust, invisible
bonds of hands and eyes, gifted by nature,
conditions of general altogether intrigue of love.

IV

54

The ground under them is a given,
so this world is a given, a gift to them.

If the world is a given it is not a gift
of certainty, given by nobody.

55

If the perfection we seek is to have no need
of divinity, then let the unknown survive

in the known. The unknown is not divine,
as the sun is not a god, though its light be perfect.

56

They know the garden elected to grow itself.
Luck planted the apple orchard.
Luck is an orange tulip, a silver birch.

They walk among the loveliness they made,
the luck they made apparent, the thought
of a garden made real in yellow and green,

and are happy. How nice to make a Paradise.
How nice to know white pansies and white peonies.
How nice, how nice. Nothing here

touching a foreign war or warring fees,
but instead a touching emphasis
on peace and the sanctuary of the seed.

57

This life cannot be right. It suffers.
Its suffering proves the injustice of existence.

Its suffering requires a saviour,
an executioner, a victim

and a comforter: the Father, the Son
and the Holy Ghost. But it is not

suffering that justifies existence.
Existence justifies suffering.

Existence is not moral or religious,
it is the game of becoming, as a child plays,

it is the question: is existence blameable
or innocent? To blame existence

is to blaspheme against the spirit of life,
of light, of innocence and play.

58

The crowds with louder and still louder voices
call for the agony of a drama ended.

Behind the scenes, in the seizing of wrists,
it is as if two laughing guards become

an altarpiece in the pink and white church
where the people gather under the arch,

obedient howls for hire, overseers
of great joy and certain destruction, disciples

of death. Weep not the abuse of it.
Afflictions are godly where all is good

and all is good on the good tree.
The godly gather around the good tree,

the belly of the fruit in folded hands,
the flesh of the fruit greatly exalted,

the deposition of the fruit,
the relaxation of the crowd.

59

He preached the measure of the gods, as his voice,
given unto us, like giving thanks, vain words,

pray for us. Sit thou here, sit here.
Many be dead. There is none. Abide in great joy.

To bury the life eternal increase of souls
alive ease down from the earth, the earth our glory,

the earth our host among heaven, redeemer of rest, rock.
Forgive among yourselves the one another.

Enjoy the company of pardon and urge
and flesh come in peace, barefoot, flesh of the rod,

flesh of the answer, flesh of the gathering,
field of the flesh, the gathered together, the looked on,

the passing, field of the tribe, the congregation,
the ground singing *God, God alone will save us.*

60

Life moves on the Plane of Matter
in shifting dynamic configurations,
the same Plane ever-changing.

The Plane is what happens on the Plane.
A single Plane with no centre,
no high or low, above or below.

All things are unique and equal on the Plane
and temporary. It is changing all the time,
but is always the Plane. It doesn't shrink or grow.

The Plane includes it all: conflict and clamour
and calm mutuality,
contest and community.

Nothing is missing on the Plane.
It lacks nothing. Nothing can be added
or taken away. It is complete and full.

The movement of matter we call death
is to be differently arranged,
differently distributed on the Plane.

All life is the life of matter, matter without form.
A formless matter of differences,
the differences that turn us on and off.

Nobody leaves the Plane. Nothing
leaves the Plane. It is here. Now.
Everything and everywhere.

There can be no spectators.
To speak of a place outside the Plane
is to speak on the Plane.

V

61

No conditioned writing, no scheme
of articulation. The rigour of play

is a universe of sweet sounds.
Accommodate yourself to this

easygoing music; the theme is
anyone talking to themselves.

What are poems but tests
in a landscape of thinking?

62

Poetry must go where prose cannot follow,
clearing domains of work in speech, in thinking
in the poem, down and down, a thought that drives itself under,

among the differences, a thought that disappears.
The knowledge of no knowledge. This is
how habits change, the surface flakes away.

The true place of matter is willingly to return
to matter, a condition of finitude and affirmation,
the figure of human destiny,

the impossibility of immortality,
and we must find in this our salvation,
becoming limitless within the limits of the mortal.

63

The poet is the living one, the one
who achieves the unknown in great and constant

concentration, who is able to live in a morning,
to be alive, kind, self-reliant,

a little absurd, to think and dream,
the haste and confusion and clamour of the clock

forgotten, to see the colours of the far-off sky
and sing in praise of day and light,

splendid daytime, splendid light of the senses,
the delight of the daylight dancing, the charm

of the dance, not forced or forcing, but fulfilled
in being itself, in being what makes it happy.

64

Poetry is intellectual delight,
conversations in which the magnificence
of a cathedral is achieved, only in words.

Every hypothesis of the future makes poetry.
Poetry is a deep speech of songs
and reverberating communication,

primordial melodies
under the hurt steps of troubled rhythms,
under the bristling impetus of desire.

65

To treat directly the thing invented, engendered
in the consciousness, endangered in the consciousness,

in corresponding co-representatives of the real,
poetry is a human voice in the mind,

constructed but ever-changing, the poem including
weather and death, the round night and flat day,

a self-parody of self-knowledge, almost seeing,
almost facing the awful absolute, the light

and warmth explicit, the intelligence of the sky,
only in poetry, the voice mingled with the song.

66

The Earth's too oblique to make out a speech on its body,
to get at the heart of whatever poetry is.

Clearly the truth in poetic form is not the truth.
We do not yet have a word for the truth in poetry.

In every respect this still obscure experience
is played as a kind of knowledge.

67

Already the unused words of the poem have fled.
The poem acknowledges their absence.

The poem makes the poem what it is,
it gives the poem its necessity,

and the poem is free, necessarily,
free to determine itself. Critics replace

the poem with its meaning. Critics say
what the poem does not say, or could not say

or did not need to say. They substitute
the poem for the commentary.

Already the poem has fled. The commentary
acknowledges the absence of the poem.

68

Relationships of drift from a childhood,
the years of simplicity that nourished,

and then beyond father and mother
the light has a public quality,

ennobling sometimes, dangerous undoubtedly,
until we acquire the acuity

required to read poetry,
to look without terror on nothingness.

The drama of yellows, blues,
reds, greens, there is nothing beyond it.

69

There is poetry and also a world
beyond poetry. Look at the scene,
a panorama of everything else:

the busy people, a swamp of subjects
strung together by propositions
and prepositions, their charming faces

in unselfconscious attitudes,
the pink, luminous face, the grey,
the brown beauty with green eyes,

the sky blue, orange, pink,
vermilion, bright yellow, violet, burgundy.
This is your brain on poetry. The weather,

flowers, faces, nudes, the people
of tomorrow, a trancelike suspension of space
and time, a dialogue with art.

70

The artificial rose is not for anything.
The rose at the window finds itself

the inhabitant of a horrible finitude
and in existence itself it finds a finitude.

But the artificial rose is called back from despair
by the window. The window arouses the rose.

There was a window before there was a rose,
in a universe it cannot open. The rose

is a replica of a rose in a replica reality
it alone makes, an art of the rose alone.

71

The book is a vision of the world. The book
corresponds to the universe. The book forgets
it is a book and thinks it is a universe.

The book imagines a future understanding
of the book. The book is a sort of guide,
but also, without doubt, a destiny.

The book does not yet know how it ends.
It does not know its author. It steps out of itself
and looks at itself through the eyes of its readers.

People who recognise themselves in the book
are already in the book. The book changes
and is new every time it is read.

From the very first pages it is clear
that the book is several books, as a new book
starts within the book. This book is the book.

The book is a rock, a porous rock full of holes.
The book has a centre of gravity and an abyss.
The book is a definition of itself.

72

A land of books, literature as equipment
for the living society, a concert of meditated values,
of mediated values, melodramas

of morality, the customs and conundrums
of writers high enough to think low,
low enough to feel high, tragicomedy,

a terror of life and death; various narratives
of abiding manners and morals, the evils of situations,
the hero's expulsion and example, elaborate plots

of circumstance and recurrent archetypes,
the strong man, the weak, virtue is vice and vice versa,
the book of conquest, the book of spectacle,

a public-private medium of plotted, clotted completion
or else street corners connected by poetry,
voice and song, a drowsy cadence, a test

of language, the poet translates the world
into a special language, a collapse of the voice,
a kind of something in the air, but what?

73

The Earth arrives before us, will leave after us,
marking time, marking the things we keep
in a climate, the Earth and its pretty morning, the gerund
of the ground grounding the forest, the private animals,
the never-seen, the for-so-long uncertain

creatures that copy themselves in impossible conditions,
mark and remark their territory. To make a beginning,
a moment of enough, anywhere, another passage
through, is to make good, is to make poetry,
is to know how to come and go.

74

A night sky full of petals, the innocent company
of stars: adolescent stars, smooth-talking,
gold-toothed stars, child stars, the single and the many,
remote in time the heat and flames.

Looking up and seeing, pulling into focus,
seeing the light established among frozen shapes,
the strange tranquillity of flame and light
hanging by a breath, the constellation of the poem.

VI

75

The moon is reticent, sober,
unobtrusive in its enforced

association with the Earth,
enforced illumination of the alternating sea.

The night has milky edges, drowsy under
a starry sky, glowing in isolation,

shatters at dawn when a car door slams.
A new beginning, a fresh start, morning.

76

The day is a pretext, an argument for saying
it is daytime, so that the day might serve a purpose,

to say what might be, to make use of it in some way.
It is daytime. It is night-time, a floating darkness.

Is today the day when the night comes? Night
for the Cosmos, the Cosmos of connections, the limit of life?

77

Ghost children in the garden,
ghost faces and ghost laughter,

throwing snowballs and making
a snowman that resembles the father.

The entangled edges of the garden
are not apparent this afternoon.

The adult world has meaning here
only as an appurtenance,

impertinence, an insult to
the god of anarchy who mocks

us with children's laughter.
If my children are happy I am happy.

78

Laughter at midday, at evening,
should make us happy. The happy should laugh,
be laughing, should find themselves in laughter.

The genesis of the joke of being,
the lost origin of the joke, belongs
to the children of the question, who still ask why.

To be still asking why, at our age,
is funny, the ultimate joke. To laugh at the joke
of being is to laugh at oneself in the question 'Why?'

79

Winter is the retreat of a world mind,
each particle part-icicle in the idiom
of the hawthorn, red winter king.

Scenes in black gardens of despair
and emptiness, white gardens of blank
ignorance, the rustle of receding histories.

The children laughing in the snow, in their boots,
physical systems in time, in unfounded being,
laugh at the snowman, the silent silver moon.

80

Prints in the snow, the snow covering the imagined
shapes of the farm, the almost home of home.
The brown horse is reconciled to declining daylight,

a stir in the air, the life and labour of the sky,
warm animal breath. The various half-covered
greenish limbs of logs, the odd way the light

lines the wood, an upright fringe of chalky colour
or dustpan colours in neglected objects arranged
in a circle of waiting. In the hills, qualities of the night.

81

The snow has many secrets. The night paints them blue
but by day they are white. The meaning of the snow
is contrived by the frozen scene. The gaps

between nature are human occasions for
occasional humans, tracing the narrow channels
and paths where self-made mountaineers

climb self-made mountains. The mountains are
giant rocks, rocks that say nothing,
but contemplate themselves in the whiteness.

There is no point complaining about
the value judgement of the mountains,
the conscious discrimination of the mountains,

their serious air, as if they were enormous answers,
as if God were a thunderclap between
one mountain and another.

82

There is pleasure in being overwhelmed by immense empty spaces
in which the landscape delights in its own developing features,

its risk and danger, our first impression of disappearing,
a passage of perspectives, freighted with landscape,

the abstract nothing manifested in our night moods,
moods of exemplary abstraction, and behind our backs

the complex last spring, final summer, autumn,
winter, eternal winter, effigies of exposure,

starry phenomena in the snow, in the doorway,
in the night of centuries, of millennia.

83

A certain ago lived a little life.
It did all that lives do. It passed like a life,
like a life lived, like lives in light contracted,
favouring light. Darkness and light
accompanied its days, making days
seem like decisions. Proximate Chronos,

short of lightning and leap, patiently waited,
concentrated on the little things
like spiders. The life and the mundane,
like fingers interlaced, withstood revelation
until the finished twilight, when light and shade
themselves are their own distance,

but, avoiding the grotto of mummified disputes,
found no superstitious accomplishment
in being alive. The warm work of living
was over, so our little life ended,
exchanging the freshness of intelligible types
for the cold, unintelligible dark.

84

A night not yet to come, still not to come,
but so ultimate it displaces the book,

the city, the development of forms,
the promise of identity. A night

against immortality, veiling the room
in the meaning of darkness, the defeat of the eye.

85

The night is committed to making the void imaginable,
the impermanence of being in incomplete
revelation; only the night seems to know
the nothing from which everything is born.

86

The last night is faceless. No moon is face enough
for the last night, the last winter, the black effervescence.

It does not speak, a night with no end, a silence
awaits the universe, the real death of everything,

the last death, the second law of thermodynamics.
The death of the universe, its indifference, its materiality,

no longer in question, no longer questioned by anyone,
all gone, all language, all thought, all desire, all existence, all presence.

We are starting, perhaps, to understand, so close to the Earth,
the sun: the love of life is creation, not for ever,

taking pleasure in the song. The absolute affirmation
is the finished song: the song that was promised has been sung.

87

There is more system in us than we would like
and less sweet spontaneity. Each of us
in a poor country of poor conflicted heads
in the morning of mankind.

If indifferent space asked us why
we carry burdens and support weights
and cannot unburden ourselves, fixed habits binding
our possibilities, what would we say?

It isn't easy to think of the cosmos beyond us.
Take a look at the night sky: you can see
all the stars. If the stars all went out we'd
be frightened. We would know it was the end.

88

The overpowering finale of the night.
The last night's conversation, the last time,
leaving no traces, no guests of the void.

The night progresses, the inner night and the outer,
the night of inaccurate accuracies, towards
the inexplicable. Every following has a fade,

every pattern an epic fail, which binds them in the same
universe, a loving emptiness, the noncircular nonresurrection
of everything, the end distracted from itself, the finitude

of finding a way, the living texture of the will,
to mark out a path for oneself, a way of being,
stopping and looking, a thought in waiting, the ambiguity

is all that matters, the moving away from certainty,
different changes in different lighting. Fade out.
Fade out to perpetual night, ending the era of light.

Fade out, fade out . . . 'All the sounds of man,
the bleating of sheep, the cries of birds,
the hum of insects, the stir that makes

the background of our lives, all that was over . . .
in another moment the pale stars alone were visible.'
In another moment the pale stars were gone.

•